DIVING AND SNORKELING GUIDE TO

The Bahamas
Nassau *and*
New Providence
Island

The Bahamas
Nassau *and*
New Providence
Island

by Steve Blount
and the editors of Pisces Books

Pisces Books ● New York

Publishers Note: At the time of publication of this book, all the information was determined to be as accurate as possible. However, when you use this guide, new construction may have changed land reference points, weather may have altered reef configurations, and some businesses may no longer be functioning. Your assistance in keeping future editions up-to-date will be greatly appreciated.
   Also, please pay particular attention to the diver rating system in this book. Know your limits!

Library of Congress Cataloging in Publication Data

Blount, Steve.
   Diving and snorkeling guide to the Bahamas.

   Includes index.
   1. Skin diving—Bahamas. 2. Bahamas—Description
and travel—1981–   I. Taylor, Herb, 1942–
II. Pisces Books (Firm) III. Title.
GV840.S78B53   1985   797.2′3′097296   85-582

ISBN 0-86636-030-1

Printed in Hong Kong

10 9 8 7 6 5 4 3 2 1

Acknowledgements

The author would especially like to thank Greg Lee of Bahamian News Service, Ltd.; Stewart Cove of Coral Harbour Divers; Stephen Darville of Westwind Villas; Joey Lulas of Underwater Tours; and Steve Sweeting and Lambert Albury of Sun Divers for their assistance in preparing this guide.

Staff

Publisher	**Herb Taylor**
Project Director	**Cora Taylor**
Managing Editor	**Steve Blount**
Editor	**Carol Denby**
Art Director	**Richard Liu**
Artist	**Daniel Kouw**

Table of Contents

How To Use This Guide

New Providence Island, one of the first stops for Spanish explorers in the New World, is now a new world for divers. This guide can help you discover that new world. In Chapter 1, you'll find an overview of New Providence and Nassau, along with information on how to get there, customs and immigration rules, shopping, sightseeing, and dining. Chapter 2 surveys the diving areas around the island and the diving operators. Chapter 3 gives detailed descriptions and photos of a variety of dive sites.

Much of the shallow ocean area surrounding New Providence has been designated a marine park by the Bahamian government. No spearfishing is allowed within the park boundaries, and the taking of live shells, corals, or other living creatures is forbidden. The marine park area is outlined on the map on page 31.

New Providence has an almost magnetic attraction for film directors. This steel wreck was deliberately sunk as a prop for the movie Never Say Never Again. ▷

The Rating System for Divers and Dives

Our suggestions as to the minimum level of expertise required for any given dive should be taken in a conservative sense, keeping in mind the old adage about there being old divers and bold divers, but few old, bold divers. We consider a *novice* to be someone in decent physical condition, who has recently completed a basic certification diving course, or a certified diver who has not been been diving recently or who has no experience in similar waters. We consider an *intermediate* diver to be a certified diver in excellent physical condition who has been diving actively for at least one year following a basic course, and who has been diving recently in similar waters. We consider an *advanced* diver to be someone who has completed an advanced certification course, has been diving recently in similar waters, and is in excellent physical condition. You will have to decide if you are capable of making any particular dive, depending on your level of training, recency of experience, and physical condition, as well as water conditions at the site. Remember that water conditions can change at any time, even during a dive. The rating system we've used is shown schematically in a chart in Chapter 3.

Thunderball Reef was the site used to film parts of the James Bond movie Thunderball.

This Spanish hogfish warily eyes the pursuing diver and oncoming photographer, typical of the area's bright tropical fish life.

1

Overview of New Providence Island

Though it has acquired the reputation of being tame and almost hum-drum among the myriad Caribbean destinations, New Providence Island is what the Caribbean was, and is, all about.

Since the time of Columbus's first landfall on San Salvador in the Bahamas, this chain has played a central role in the history of the Western Hemisphere.

Called *baja mar*, or "shallow sea," by the Spanish, the islands were the gateway to the New World for more than 300 years.

The *baja mar* is one of the world's great maritime highways. Spanish galleons loaded with the wealth of the Indies, pirates and privateers, boatloads of colonists, great military armadas, wolfpacks of U-boats, and sleek cruise ships have all passed this way.

The earliest memories of an emerging New World live on in these islands. From the wharves of New Providence Island, supplies and trade goods moved to the colonies. Here cotton was traded for gunpowder by the blockade runners of the Civil War era, and rum runners loaded their wares during Prohibition. They live also in the historical sites of New Providence, such as Rawson Square where a statue of Queen Victoria overlooks the markets and streets of old Nassau. And they live in the local architecture, from the Government House to the high-tech hotels and office buildings that mark Nassau's emergence as an international center of offshore banking.

Though the thriving financial industry steadily increases, making tourists happy is the central and dominant business of the Bahamas. And New Providence is not only the political capital, it is the chief tourist center as well. About 1.7 million visitors entered the Bahamas in 1982, and almost a million of them went to Nassau.

Many of these tourists found Nassau and New Providence a satisfying compromise between the seclusion of an island vacation and the excitement of visiting a metropolitan center. But the sheer volume of visitors has tended to make serious divers discount the island's diving potential. In some folks' minds, a place that attracts a million people a year can't have virgin diving. They're wrong.

Windsurfing is another of Nassau's aquatic pleasures. The broad, shallow bays of the island's north side are the best places to run with the gentle trade winds. ⟱

Ironically, the dive resort building boom that went off in the Caribbean in the early 1970s bypassed New Providence altogether. But not because the diving isn't good. Many of those resorts were partially financed with aid from government development funds. Because of its booming tourist business, New Providence isn't the kind of place a government would spend public funds to develop diving. Most governments regard diving as a marginal tourist industry. Also, because diving is a marginal business when compared to general tourism, businesses on New Providence didn't make a special effort to attract divers. The islands that put the most emphasis on developing diving were largely those that had a small base of tourists to begin with, and fewer activities to attract tourists.

The result has been that, while some of the places that were virgin dive areas in the early 1970s have had their reefs stomped on and jet-finned into coral dust, the bare trickle of divers going into New Providence has left much of the island's submarine scenery pristine. This is particularly true of dive sites on the west and south sides of the island.

By plane or by boat, nearly a million visitors flood Nassau each year. The cruise ships dock at Prince George's Wharf in Nassau Harbour. The downtown area and historic district are just behind the Wharf.

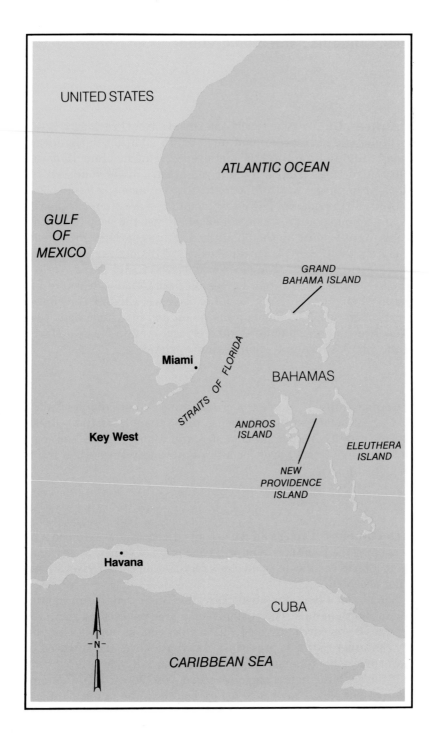

Centered in the Eastern Caribbean, the Bahamas are the dry tops of a vast, shallow undersea plain called the Bahamas Bank.

Airlines. Unlike some Caribbean islands, New Providence is served by a multitude of international airlines. In addition to the large selection of flights from the U.S. or Europe, frequent promotions result in very attractive airfares. Even if you always make your own reservations, it might be worth talking to a travel agent before booking a flight to New Providence. The promotional fares are often package deals that are complex, and it takes an expert to get the very best price. If you just want to pick up the phone and get a seat, New Providence is served from the U.S. by American Airlines, Bahamasair, Delta Airlines, Eastern Airlines, Pan American World Airways, and Trans World Airlines. Air Canada flies direct to Nassau from Canada. If you're in the mood for a slightly different aerial experience, Chalk's International Airlines offers seaplane flights from Miami and Ft. Lauderdale, Florida to New Providence. The planes take off and land in Nassau Harbour, and the Chalk's terminal is on Paradise Island.

Cruise ships. A number of cruise ships call at Nassau. Talk to a travel agent before trying the cruise lines, though, as their standard packages usually include just one day and night in port. You may be able to arrange to stay over for a few days and return when the boat next stops in port.

Documents. If you're an American citizen, you won't need a passport to enter the Bahamas. You will need proof of your U.S. citizenship, such as a birth certificate or a voter's registration card. Driver's licenses are not accepted.

The obvious cautions about carrying illicit drugs and handguns apply to the Bahamas. The customs folks are real serious about drugs and guns. If you carry any medication with you, be sure it's in a pharmacy container with the prescription still attached. It's rumored to be almost impossible to get a permit to bring in a handgun.

If you're flying home, on your return, you'll clear U.S. Customs at the airport in New Providence before boarding the plane. Things can get a little crowded on Fridays and Sundays, so leave some extra time and be prepared to wait in line. Once you go through U.S. Customs, you'll be directed to a departure lounge, and you can't leave it without clearing Customs all over again.

Hotels, Dining, and Shopping

At this writing, only one hotel offered dive packages. Coral Harbour Divers has an arrangement with the Casaurinas Hotel, which is located outside of Nassau on the north side of the island. Again, check with a travel agent for the best prices. There are a lot of hotel rooms on the island, and someone's always running a promotional package.

The biggest decision will be whether to stay on Paradise Island, in Nassau proper, or in the Cable Beach area. Paradise Island and Cable Beach are the priciest. If you're staying on Paradise Island, it will take a little longer to get over to Lyford Cay to dive the south side of the island. On the other hand, if you're going to put in one or two dives during the trip, and would be happy on a shallow, fishy reef, the areas around Athol Island are easily reached from Paradise Island.

The food in the hotels is generally pretty good, but many of the hotel restaurants are fairly expensive, about $20 per person for dinner. There is a McDonald's (located in the shopping arcade of the Sheraton British Colonial) and a Lum's on Bay Street. Captain Nemo's, a seafood restaurant on east Bay Street, serves good food at a reasonable price. Also, there are a number of small eateries, such as the Delaporte Bar on the north coast highway near Delaporte Point, where you can get Bahamian-style seafood very cheaply. Dinner for four at the Delaporte is about $20 total.

Nassau has something else many diving locations lack, gourmet restaurants. The Graycliff, on West Hill Street near Government House in Nassau, is one. The food is superb, but if you think the hotel restaurants are expensive, wait until you peruse Graycliff's menu. Bring your American Express Gold Card or be prepared to trade your Rolex for dinner.

Shopping. Nothing originates in the Bahamas, so there are very few true shopping bargains. Bay Street in Nassau is the shopping district, lined with small but elegant stores offering perfumes from Europe and America, electronics from Japan, or diamonds and emeralds from South America. Most of these items can be bought in the U.S. at comparable prices.

The straw market on Bay Street does offer something a bit different. If it can be made out of raffia or straw, you'll find it in this open-air arcade. Hundreds of craftspeople jam the area, offering rugs, hats, purses, and dolls, as well as shell jewelry and wood carvings. Remember to haggle, the first price you're offered is probably double the real selling price.

History and Sightseeing

The Bahamas were initially discovered by a race of Indians, the Lucayans. Most likely, they were a branch of the Arawaks, a race of South American people that migrated up the Indies from the Orinoco River basin. During this journey up the archipelago, the Arawaks were just one step ahead of another group, the Caribs.

The Caribs, for whom the Caribbean Sea was named, were cannibals. From their homes in the lower Indies, they raided Arawak villages on Hispaniola, Cuba, the Virgin Islands, and in the Bahamas. Although they carried off men and women as slaves, reportedly killing those they couldn't carry with them, their efforts were paltry compared to those of the Europeans. The Lucayans of the Bahamas were used to work gold mines on Hispaniola, and less than a generation after the discovery of the Bahamas by Columbus, there were no more Lucayans.

The Europeans. By 1646, the English, well established on Bermuda to the north, considered the Bahamas as Crown property. Land grants were made to encourage colonizations. But the islands, all rock and sand with little fertile soil, were hard on men and animals.

Paradise Island is a primary focus of activity. The Resorts International casino, hotel, and convention center complex also includes gourmet restaurants, a discotheque, and show theatre. Marinas, shopping, and a seaplane terminal make Paradise Island almost a self-contained resort.

The first major industry to succeed was *wrecking*, the practice of salvaging wrecked merchant ships.

These salvors were not above occasionally extinguishing the light in a lighthouse, or building a fire far inland to lure ships onto the shallow reefs of the Bahama Bank.

In addition to the wreckers, Nassau was for several decades the lair of some of the hemisphere's most desperate pirates. During the periodic wars that flared between England, France, and Spain in the 17th and 18th centuries, the English often granted sea captains the right to pillage enemy shipping without being subject to a charge of piracy. These private naval vessels, or privateers, were not quick to give up sacking Spanish or French ships when a truce was declared.

Nassau became the home port of many of these rascals. In fact, during the War of the Spanish Succession and for four years afterward, from 1703 until 1714, Nassau was governed by the pirates. Edward Teach, remembered as Blackbeard, was one of the most prominent.

After numerous complaints from the Spanish, England sent a naval hero, Captain Woodes Rogers, to evict the pirates. His accomplishment is commemorated by the street in front of Prince George's Wharf, now called Woodes Rogers Walk.

Smuggling has a prominent place in the modern history of the Bahamas as well. During Prohibition in the U.S., liquor from Europe was shipped to Nassau, where it was transferred to freighters, airplanes, and fast coastal boats. The ragtag flotilla deceived, outran, or outfought the Coast Guard, bringing load after load of alcoholic libations to the speakeasies of a thirsty America.

The government of the Bahamas profited as handsomely as the rumrunners. It doubled its tax on liquor imports. Every case that came through Nassau deposited a hefty sum in the colony's coffers. Massive public works projects, including Prince George's Wharf, where the cruise ships now dock, and the municipal water tower, were built with liquor tax revenues.

Some farsighted businessmen saw in this new wealth a way for the islands to become self sufficient. Wealthy Americans had begun spending the winter season in Nassau at the turn of the century. Now, with the liquor revenues, the capital was available to build facilities to better serve these tourists and to advertise to attract more. The Bahamas was thus set on the path it still follows. The heavy liquor tax was eventually repealed, but rising revenues from tourism encouraged Great Britain to consider the colony self sufficient, and in 1973, the Bahamas became independent under the leadership of Prime Minister Lynden O. Pindling.

An enjoyable day can be spent in visiting the cluster of historic sites and buildings which trace the history of Nassau. An excellent guide to the historic district, Pictorial Nassau, is available at newsstands and bookstores all over the island.

2

Diving in New Providence Island

When divers talk about the shrines of scuba, Nassau—located on New Providence Island in the Bahamas—is not normally mentioned.

However, if you've seen any of the numerous James Bond movies with underwater scenes (*Thunderball, Dr. No,* and *Never Say Never Again* among others), or if you remember the TV series *Flipper*, then you've already seen what diving around New Providence is like. New Providence has been a popular underwater location for major motion pictures. Parts of *Splash!* were filmed here, as was *Wet Gold*, which starred Brooke Shields. Underwater sequences for *Cocoon*, set for release in late 1985, were filmed here as well.

The filmmakers come because New Providence is close to the U.S. and is easy to reach via scheduled airlines. Also, because there are direct flights from major U.S. cities, the airfare is comparatively low. The weather is dependable, very good during most of the year, and there's always a lee where work can continue if the wind does kick up for a day or two. And one more reason: There's some very good diving.

On the north side of the island, very close to Nassau, there are shallow reefs and several outstanding wrecks: the *Mahoney*, the *Alcora*, and the *LCT*. On the south side is an excellent wall, the Clifton Wall, with a dozen shallow and deep sites clustered within a mile of each other. These are things any visiting diver can count on seeing. There are other sites too, farther out, wilder, less visited. These sites are not a sure thing and depend on the vagaries of weather, availability of fast boats, and the presence of other experienced divers. Whichever side of New Providence you see, the close and familiar or the far away, be prepared to shock your diving peers when you return from your vacation with stories of deep walls, huge sponges, mammoth groupers, plentiful lobsters, and a half-dozen movie sets. They won't believe you saw all of that in New Providence. But remember you have proof—just tell them to watch for the reruns of *Thunderball*.

Sponges, mounding corals, and deepwater gorgonians decorate the vertical edges of the Clifton Wall, along the south shore of New Providence. ⃗

North Side Diving

Nassau is located on the north side of New Providence, and most of the major hotels are here or on Paradise Island, slightly east and north of Nassau proper. Nassau and the Paradise Island hotels are the center of action, with restaurants, nightclubs, and shops clustered around the harbor area.

The diving most convenient to these hotels is also on the north side. Most of the sites here are either shallow coral gardens or wrecks. The two operators located on the north side, Sun Divers and Bahama Divers, don't often dive on the south side—it's a 45-minute run from the harbor and, with any wind at all, a rough ride. Primarily, they stick to the north side sites. When the wind blows, they dive the shallows in the lee of Athol Island and Rose Island.

Bahamas Divers is located on east Bay Street, very near the foot of the Paradise Island Bridge. The shop has a fairly complete selection of gear for sale or rent. Instruction can be arranged, either a full course or quick familiarization, and they offer the same basic services as Sun Divers. Bahamas Divers docks their two boats at the marina at the north end of the Paradise Island Bridge, just to the left of the toll booths on Paradise Island.

As with Sun Divers, most of the trips are to sites on the north side—the shallows near Athol Island or the various wrecks and reefs fronting Paradise Island.

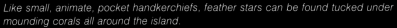

Like small, animate, pocket handkerchiefs, feather stars can be found tucked under mounding corals all around the island.

The LCT Wreck on the north side of New Providence offers a spectacular first wreck dive to novices and beautiful coral growth for the more experienced.

Sun Divers operates from a small hut on the beach at the Sheraton British Colonial Hotel. Their boats leave the Sheraton dock daily at 9 a.m. for a single-tank dive, and at 1 p.m. for a two-tank dive. On the way out to the site they pick up divers from docks around the harbor and at Paradise Island.

The operation is owned by Steve Sweeting and Lambert Albury. You can usually find them at the hut before the morning dive, or just before the afternoon dive leaves. They have a 30-foot inboard with 12½-foot beam, wide and easy riding in a swell. There's plenty of room to gear up on the stern and stride off the swim step, or you can roll off the gunwale if you prefer.

For novices or non-divers, Sun Divers offers a pool check-out followed by a dive, all gear included, for one price. The dives are the same price whether you bring your own gear or use theirs.

Sun Divers also caters to snorkelers, especially on trips to the shallows around Athol Island. If you go during "the season," November to April, they'll likely have two boats running daily, and you'll get a choice of dive sites and companions.

Underwater Tours is a specialty operation on east Bay Street. Owner Joey Lulas takes very limited groups to a selection of private north side sites, including the wreck of the *Alcora*. If private guided tours interest you, be sure to contact him well in advance of your visit to make arrangements.

Coral Harbour Divers is not actually located at Coral Harbour—the shop is at Lyford Cay, on the extreme western end of New Providence. The operation is owned and run by Stewart Cove and his wife, Tulla. Ordinarily, they run the sites on the south side of the island, from the Lyford Cay dropoff around Goulding Cay to Clifton Wall. There are some sites farther out—a 25-minute run in Cove's 24-foot Seacraft boat. These sites are really diveable only when the ocean is flat.

Most trips are run in a beamy 32-footer with center tank racks and plenty of dry storage below deck for your odds and ends. The Clifton Wall sites are only 10 minutes from the dock at Lyford Cay and, depending on the number of divers, Cove will operate up to four boats.

For divers staying in town, Coral Harbour's bus picks up divers and their gear around 8:15 a.m. and ferries them out to the shop for the 9 a.m. dive. If you're planning on doing a lot of diving, it might make sense to investigate Coral Harbour's hotel/dive packages, which they run in conjunction with Casuarinas Hotel, about 10 minutes from Lyford Cay.

As this guide was going to press, Coral Harbour was the only operation offering hotel packages.

Shallow turtle grass flats are the best place to spot starfish. The slow-moving echinoderms can often be found grazing the bottom between small coral heads.

The sponges of New Providence, especially those on the south side of the island, are comparable to those found in other great diving areas of the Caribbean.

As do Sun Divers and Bahamas Divers, Coral Harbour offers full instructional services. Their new shop at the marina, with full classroom and easy access to open water, makes them a good choice for lessons if you want a full course. Truly novice divers who don't want to take instructions might be more comfortable with Sun Divers or Bahamas Divers, as Coral Harbour tends more toward longer and deeper reef trips for more experienced folk.

For more information, you may want to write or call the operations before you make final reservations.

Bahamas Divers
P.O. Box 5004
Nassau, Bahamas
809-323-2644

Sun Divers
P.O. Box N10728
Nassau, Bahamas
809-322-3301

Coral Harbour Divers
P.O. Box SS6635
Nassau, Bahamas
809-326-4171

Underwater Tours
P.O. Box N1658
Nassau, Bahamas
809-322-3285

Conservation and the Bahamas Marine Park

It is the obligation of every diver to minimize their impact on the undersea environment. Although every dive inevitably results in some disruption or even damage to the dive area, being aware of a few simple principles will make you a better diver and less of a risk to the playground beneath the sea.

Buoyancy. The most obvious, but least understood, principle is to remain neutrally buoyant. Neutral buoyancy means just that. A diver wearing the right amount of weight, with just a puff of air in their buoyancy compensator, will neither rise nor sink. While neutrally buoyant, the diver can hover over, rather than crawl through, growth on the seafloor. Although coral looks very solid, it is in fact the fragile tissue of living animals. Dangling depth gauges and octopus regulators can bang into hard corals, killing polyps or producing scars which may become infected with coral-killing sponge or algae. Hoses and straps can also get tangled in soft corals, uprooting them or tearing their plumes. Nothing is so destructive as a herd of overly heavy divers scrambling and scraping over a reef. Don't hesitate to ask the advice of a dive guide about how much weight to wear.

Flippers. Watch those fin tips. The big power fins favored by most divers act like a McCormack reaper when churned by a pair of human legs. It's incredibly easy to break off the tips of branching corals or edges of sheet corals by thrashing them with jet fins. While diving, be aware that your feet actually end about 12 inches beyond your toes, at the edge of your fins. Also be careful not to get so close to the sand that you kick it up off the bottom. Besides ruining the visibility for everyone else on the dive, the sand can settle on corals, making their tenuous lives that much more difficult. If you want to get down in the sand to observe something, look around to ensure you have a clear area to settle down. Go in vertically, like a landing helicopter, and touch the sand gently or hover just above its surface. When you're ready to move on, don't just kick off. Instead, inhale to give yourself extra buoyancy and use your hand to push away from the bottom before kicking with your fins.

Fishery Laws of the Bahamas

The government of the Bahamas has taken a number of steps to preserve and protect the islands' ocean resources. The laws listed here are those that most concern divers, but are by no means a comprehensive list. If you plan to fish extensively while in New Providence, you may want to write the Ministry of Tourism for a complete copy of fishing regulations. Particularly if you plan on spearfishing, you will want to know the laws. No spearfishing of any sort is allowed while using scuba, and powered spearguns are not allowed into the country. If you put a powered speargun in your luggage, it's very likely the Bahamian customs officials will impound it.

- No poisons may be used to catch or kill fish.

- No marine animals or products may be taken with the use of underwater breathing equipment.

- Hawaiian slings or pole spears are the only type of spearing devices snorkel divers may use. Powered spearguns may not be used.

- The export of any marine animal or product is illegal unless a permit has been obtained.

- No marine animals or products may be removed from the north coast of New Providence from Goulding Cay in the west to a line drawn between the eastern tip of Athol Island and the eastern end of New Providence, and inside of a line drawn through the fringing islands. In the Exuma Cays Land and Sea Park no commercial fishing is allowed.

3

New Providence Dive Sites

The sites around New Providence fall into three basic categories: shallow reefs, deeper reefs and walls, and wrecks. Due to the generally benign water conditions around the island, most of the sites are accessible to divers at any level of experience.

The chart (page 30) does recommend some dives, mostly the deeper and wall dives only for more experienced divers. With proper supervision, many of these are suitable for novices as well.

There is very little opportunity for unsupervised shore diving around New Providence. Most of the sites are too far from shore to swim to. Although this may not suit the most ardent four-dive-per-day diver, the boat rides are short and pleasant. The boats in use by the operators are generally fast, comfortable, and well set up for diving. The boat diving also contributes to the admirable safety record of the island's dive operators, as there is a guide along on virtually every dive done by visitors.

If you haven't been diving in the past year, or if you think your skills might be a little rusty, talk to the dive operators. They don't expect everyone who comes to New Providence to be an expert diver. They're used to helping refresh people's memories. You'll be more comfortable and have a better vacation if you let the operators do what you're paying them to do—help.

Although it shines brilliantly when lit by a photographer's strobe, even the brightest sponge looks grayish when viewed without artificial light. The sponges of New Providence are so varied and colorful, it's worth carrying a flashlight to reveal their true colors. ▷

	Novice Diver	Novice w/Instructor or divemaster	Intermediate Diver	Intermediate w/Instructor or divemaster	Advanced diver	Advanced diver w/Instructor or divemaster
South Side						
1 Clifton Wall	×	×	×	×	×	
2 The Chute	×	×	×	×	×	
3 Never Say Never Again Wreck		×	×	×	×	
4 20,000 Leagues*		×	×	×	×	
5 Porpoise Pens	×	×	×	×	×	
North Side						
6 LCT Wreck*	×	×	×	×	×	
7 Trinity Caves		×	×	×	×	
8 Mahoney Wreck		×	×	×	×	
9 Thunderball Reef	×	×	×	×	×	
10 Alcora Wreck		×	×	×	×	
11 Balmoral Island*	×	×	×	×	×	

*Denotes good snorkeling spots

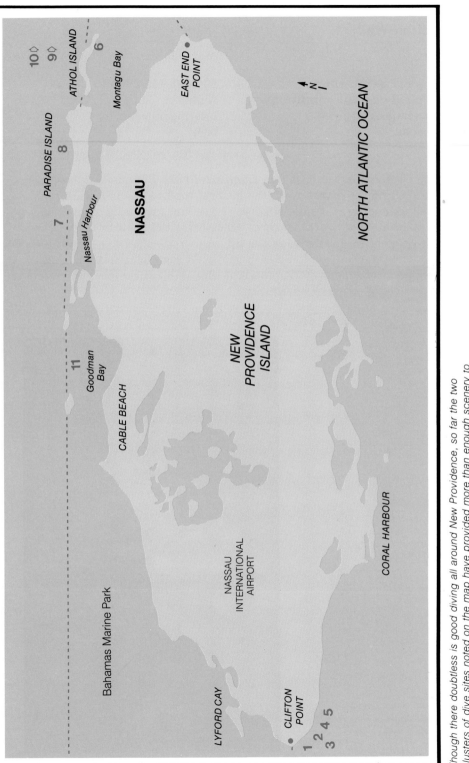

Though there doubtless is good diving all around New Providence, so far the two clusters of dive sites noted on the map have provided more than enough scenery to keep visitors busy.

Clifton Wall   1

Typical depth range   :   50-90 ft. (15-28 m)
Typical current conditions :   slight
Expertise required   :   intermediate
Access   :   boat

The Clifton Wall is host to a number of New Providence's best dive sites. Clifton is a true wall; the general topography is a wide, sandy shelf extending ½-1 mile offshore (1-1½ km) gradually sloping down to 40 or 50 feet. Scattered coral heads litter the shelf for 20-30 yards (18-28 meters) shoreward of the lip.

The lip of the wall varies in depth. At some places it's as shallow as 45 feet (13 meters). At others, it dips to 80 or 90 feet (28 meters) before going entirely vertical.

The Clifton Wall is a vertical escarpment of mounding coral that runs nearly a third the length of New Providence about a half mile off the south shore.

Knots of sponge colonies are common along the Clifton Wall. This tangle includes at least three species: a large basket, purple tubes, and red, purple, and yellow rope sponges.

Most of the coral is of the encrusting forms—star, mountainous star, and sheet corals—and the growth is impressive. The lip is riddled with crevices, undercuts, ledges, and chutes. Large tube sponges, especially yellow tubes, dangle into these declivities. Vase and basket sponges are also spotted around the lip and edge of the dropoff. The wall has a truly impressive number of rope sponges, again the yellow-green ones predominating over red and purple. There are very few large sea fans, but other forms of soft coral—sea whips, sea plumes, deepwater gorgonians—are plentiful.

Although the area is fished fairly heavily, large tropicals abound. At an unnamed site opposite the Porpoise Pens, two of the largest gray angels that ever graced a Caribbean reef are regular performers.

The wall attracts a lot of groupers, from big ones up to 4 or 5 feet (1.5 meters) to smaller ones of about a foot (0.3 meter) in length. All varieties can be seen, too; from monster blackfin and marble groupers down to shoebox-sized coneys, Nassaus, and tigers.

Other large pelagics are often seen here, as well. The occasional shark is joined by larger numbers of big rays. Smaller Southern stingrays park in the gullies between the shallow patch reefs, so watch those flippers on the shallow dives.

A striking feature of this area is the sheer size and variety of the animals. They aren't hand-fed, so they're a little skittish, but by patiently stalking you should be able to get close enough for a decent photo.

Animals that filter their food from the water thrive in the rich current that sweeps along the edge of the Clifton Wall.

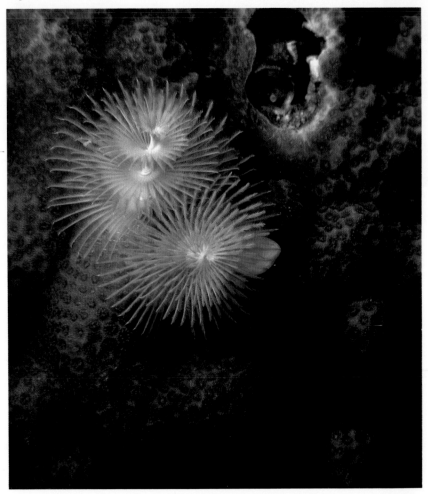

A distant relative of the graceful starfish, the sea cucumber may be the most unsightly member of the vast echinoderm family. Photo: H. Taylor.

The whole catalog of Caribbean tropicals is represented here, either near the wall or in the shallows just shoreward. In a few outings you'll see tang, bar jacks, Spanish hogfish, hog snappers, yellowtails, graysbys, rock beauties, French-striped grunts, squirrelfish, damsels, trumpetfish, diamond blennies, royal grammas, porkfish, spadefish, spotted butterflyfish, French angels, gobies, sea cucumbers; basically whatever you're looking for.

A lot of cleaning activity goes on here, as well. Tiger groupers at cleaning stations are very approachable, and while you might not be able to fill the frame of your 1:1 macro framer with a goby working over the lower lip of a coney, try using a 28mm or 35mm lens on your Nikonos for some head-and-fins shots.

Generally, the visibility on the wall is good, ranging from 50 feet (15 meters) in windy weather right on up to 150 feet (50 meters) or more.

The Chute 2

Typical depth range   :   50-90 ft. (15-28 m)
Typical current conditions :   slight
Expertise required   :   intermediate
Access   :   boat

Along the Clifton Wall is a site called the Chute—a large crevasse in the wall with sand spilling through. The lip of the wall is shallow here, about 40 feet (12 meters). The Chute is a vast trough, 20 feet (6 meters) deep and at least 20 feet wide. It breaches the mounding-coral lip and continues down into the abyss.

On the west side is an overhang and two tunnels which are just big enough for a smallish diver to crawl through. The tunnels join under the reef and exit through a chimney about 15 feet (5 meters) long onto the top of the reef.

Sand falls, such as the Chute, are formed by similar, though opposite forces to those which create gullies on land. Gullies are created by uncontrolled water runoff while sand falls are formed on steep underwater slopes by sand constantly moving over the edge of a cliff. This movement prevents reef building animals from taking hold and creating a barrier to hold back the sand.

A nest of purple, red, and yellow rope sponges near the Chute displays a variety matched by few Caribbean destinations except Jamaica.

Be careful going through the Chute area, as the sand bottom is very fine and loose. Use the cave diver's technique of jabbing two fingers into the sand and pulling yourself through, rather than using fins, so as not to silt out the Chute and tunnel for those behind you.

Use buoyancy to rise through the chimney, and watch your tank on the ceiling of the cave. Tank valves can do a number on the thin edges of plate corals that overlap into the tunnel.

If you're the first diver in the Chute, check out the chimney and entrance to the cave. The critters think it's a pretty neat place, too. You may find a luxury-sized grouper or perhaps some squirrelfish lounging about before the humans come.

Typical depth range	:	30-50 ft. (10-15 m)
Typical current conditions	:	none
Expertise required	:	novice
Access	:	boat

The story line of the last James Bond film, *Never Say Never Again,* called for a wreck. The crew found a terrific 110-foot (34-meter) freighter. It has a beautiful rounded pilothouse up forward, a short bow, a long cabin with easy access, a broad fantail, and plenty of hatches—in short, it's a perfect wreck. Seized as a dope runner by the Bahamian government, the boat was sunk here by the film crew with the help of Coral Harbour owner Stewart Cove.

Large groupers are very common in the area of the wheelhouse of the Never Say Never Again *wreck.*

Unlike the wrecks on the north side of New Providence, this steel wreck hasn't had time to develop a full coating of marine growth. Still, the nearly intact freighter is a stunning shallow water wreck dive.

Sitting upright in 50 feet (15 meters) of water on a sand bottom, the boat is easily viewed from the surface. From the top it looks small, but once you're down the size begins to impress. Being the first one down will ensure a silt-free photo of the wheelhouse, as most divers tend to crawl, rather than float, through the large, glassless windows. The algae now covering the wreck holds a lot of sand, and it doesn't take much to kick it up. If you're a serious photographer, take a model and try to get out on the wreck with as few other divers as possible. It's the single most photogenic wreck in this part of the Caribbean. That's more than just one man's opinion; three television commercials and yet another full-length feature—*Wet Gold*—were filmed on this wreck.

If silt becomes a problem, move to the west side and look back toward the boat. About amidships, the remains of a wooden dinghy protrude from the sand. With a wide-angle lens, you can take in the graceful curve of the dinghy's sides, the entire wreck, and dozens of garden eels waving in the sand between.

A few dozen yards away are the remains of the airplane prop created for *Thunderball*. The script called for a jet fighter armed with

These squirrelfish, like squirrelfish the world over, are shy creatures which prefer night to day. Their large eyes help them see in the dark.

Though it looks like an overgrown schoolyard jungle gym, this was actually one of the sets used in the James Bond thriller Thunderball.

nuclear missiles to be hijacked and hidden on the sea floor. The "fighter" was made from steel pipes and fiberglass. The skin is now gone, leaving what appears to be a huge erector set. Every square inch of the frame is carpeted with gorgonians, giving the effect of a fuzzy set of monkey bars.

Large basket stars cling to the gorgonians. To one side of the airplane is an enormous clump of brain coral. The fish here are fed pretty regularly and are more tame. A green anemone with tentacles as big around as your thumb lives in one of the side pockets of the coral head.

Typical depth range	:	15-25 ft. (5-8 m)
Typical current conditions	:	none
Expertise required	:	novice
Access	:	boat

One of the inshore dives off the Clifton Wall is called 20,000 Leagues Under the Sea, after the movie of the same name.

20,000 Leagues is a coral garden with a difference. The spur-and-groove reef here is very well developed, with the walls of the spurs reaching up 10 feet (3 meters) from the sand channels between. These channels are, in places, so narrow a diver has a hard time squeezing through. The channels twist and wind in an almost serpentine pattern.

The narrow gullies of the shallow 20,000 Leagues area abound with brilliant tropicals, such as this queen angel. Photo: H. Taylor.

Though shallow, 20,000 Leagues is subject to very little surge. The calm water and small life forms that infest the crevices make it an excellent spot for macrophotography.

By following the bottom, you get an impression of what it must be like to fly through the Grand Canyon in a helicopter.

The fish life here is the attraction. Small tropicals mob the many crevices, and larger game—particularly Nassau groupers—park for a rest in the undercuts at the base of the spurs. The area is visited sometimes by large leopard rays and jumbo blackfin groupers.

The whole patch must encompass several acres, and it runs almost all of the way out to the edge of the wall. If you're a photographer, try lying on your back or sitting down in one of the sand channels while divers swim over the tops of the spurs. Light the sides of the spur and the divers with a strobe and you'll get something that resembles a good wall shot, only with more light and brighter water.

Typical depth range	:	40-90 ft. (12-28 m)
Typical current conditions	:	none
Expertise required	:	novice
Access	:	boat

This spot is just opposite the pens where the underwater sequences for *Flipper* were filmed. The pens are still in the water, adjacent to the shore, and were used last year for the underwater sequences of *Cocoon*. Ric O'feldman—diver, amateur cetologist, and part-time filmmaker—trained and worked with Flipper, but for this movie, several porpoises were caught in Exuma and a trainer was brought in from the Florida Keys.

The Porpoise Pens area is just offshore from an underwater corral that was used to film sequences for the TV series Flipper and parts of the movie Cocoon. Photo: H. Taylor

A fabulous black coral bush clings to an outcropping on the wall at Porpoise Pens. Black coral jewelry is available in Nassau, and though it can legally be imported into the U.S., conscientious divers won't encourage the abuse of this resource by buying it.

The Porpoise Pens is a deep dive along the wall, with the lip beginning at about 40 feet (12 meters) and a lot of the scenery at 70 to 80 feet (22 to 25 meters).

At these depths, the true dimensions of the wall are apparent. Inky blue-blackness laps at your fins from below. On the wall, as if displayed in a submarine gallery, are splash after splash of aquatic art: a swirling deepwater gorgonian recalling Van Gogh, a pastiche of encrusting sponge fetching up images of Jackson Pollock.

Although black coral jewelry is sold in various shops on the island, it doesn't appear as though this part of the reef has been stripped of the semi-precious stuff. There are several bushes located in the 70 foot (22 meter) range here.

Be careful with your depth gauge. It's very easy to get excited by an oversized sponge, or be enticed into diving after a grouper and end up at 110 feet plus plus plus. The divemasters on New Providence are safety conscious and will give you full information about each dive before you enter the water. But if you have any question about your own skills, stick close to the dive leader. He'll probably be able to show you the better parts of the reef, as well.

LCT Wreck 6

Typical depth range	:	10-20 ft. (3-6 m)
Typical current conditions	:	none
Expertise required	:	novice
Access	:	boat

The LCT wreck is a World War II-vintage LST that was used to ferry freight back and forth to Exuma in the years after the war. While making its way out of Nassau Harbour, it began taking on water. The crew ran it aground to try to salvage the cargo, and it settled into its present position, just on the southwest side of Athol Island.

The water over the top of the wheelhouse is only knee deep, and it's about 20 feet (6 meters) to the sand. The boat is fairly intact.

Look closely under the keel of the LCT Wreck and you may find a tiny arrow crab, like this one, nestled among the hard and soft corals.

A piece of the wreckage, perhaps part of the engine, lies a few yards behind the LCT wreck. The metal is liberally coated with encrusting sponge and soft corals. Small tropicals may be found inside.

Although LSTs are not the most exciting wrecks to look at, this one is fun, partly because of the sea fans and rope sponges rooted to its decks, and the presence of large fish.

The decks and doorways are pretty well coated with fire coral, so wear a wetsuit or be careful.

The forward cabin is pretty open, and there's a cable coiled up on the floor. With the light flooding in through gaping holes in the sides and top, it makes a nice photo with a strobe or with available light. The north side of the wreck has a knob of brain coral the size of a bowling ball growing on one of the gunwales. Try getting in close to this with a wide-angle lens and light it with your strobe.

Behind and to the south of the wreck is a large, square, boxlike affair. With a wide angle lens, this will fill the front of your film frame, and the wreck can be seen in the background.

Look in the sand underneath the stern. You may find any assortment of large or small tropicals hiding in the sponge, algae and coral piled up in the shadows where the prop used to be.

Typical depth range	:	45 ft. (14 m)
Typical current conditions	:	light
Expertise required	:	intermediate
Access	:	boat

The caves are due north of the Club Med beach on Paradise Island. The name is misleading; actually there is a quintet of grottoes, not a trio. In addition to the three main caves, there are two smaller ones a few hundred feet to the west.

Large groupers are very common in the area of Trinity Caves. Though the area lacks abundant hard coral, soft corals are plentiful, and the cave walls are covered with encrusting growth. Photo.

A coney, hovering just in front of the fantastic variegated background of Trinity Caves, is caught in the middle of a color change. Like a chameleon lizard on land, these groupers can change their colors at will to better blend with their environment.

The reef here is mostly limestone, with abundant soft corals—gorgonians and sea fans—but little hard coral. There's a large stand of rare pillar coral, though. Tube worms cover the surface of the rocks, which is carpeted with calcareous algae.

This site might be called the Spiny Lobster Sheraton; the crevices and small holes in the limestone substrate are literally crawling with lobsters. However, this is definitely not the place to dive for dinner. Trinity Caves is part of the area protected from hunting and collecting of any sort.

The caves are coated with a thick lining of sponges and other encrusting growth. Clusters of purple and brown tube sponges, green rope sponges, and whip corals dangle from the walls and ceilings.

Big animals are often spotted near the caves. Large groupers are seen often, and rays with 6-foot wingspans aren't uncommon.

Typical depth range	:	45 ft. (14 m)
Typical current conditions	:	moderate to heavy
Expertise required	:	intermediate
Access	:	boat

The *Mahoney* is something of a mystery. Interestingly, the boat's name was never *Mahoney,* and no one seems to know why it's called that now. The ship was a 212-foot (64 meter) steel freighter that went down in the hurricane of 1929. It broke in two while sinking, and the stern and the bow are now about 100 yards (90 meters) apart.

The wreck was dynamited flat to prevent other ships from hitting it, so there isn't a great deal of relief to the wreck.

When dive guides start their fish feeding routine, the first animals in are often enormous horse-eyed jacks. These big, bullish-looking fish are fast, strong, and aggressive.

Though it was blasted flat so as not to interfere with shipping, the Mahoney *can still be recognized beneath the encrusting growth.*

The steam boiler, located off to the southwest side of the main wreckage, was left intact. It's heavily encrusted with fire coral (watch those ungloved hands) and is a marvelous photographic prop.

The fish here are photogenic as well. They're accustomed to being fed, and are a little tamer than at many other sites around the island.

The substrate around the *Mahoney* is littered with gorgonians and other soft corals.

Normally, the operators only dive the *Mahoney* at slack tide, as there's a fast current over the wreck when the tide is moving, and especially on a falling tide.

Typical depth range	:	25 ft. (8 m)
Typical current conditions	:	light
Expertise required	:	novice
Access	:	boat

You've doubtless already seen this reef—this is where the speargun sequence in *Thunderball* was filmed. It's worth seeing in person, though. The area is a large patch-reef complex with numerous brain and star coral heads. The reef is long and narrow, and runs north and south, perpendicular to New Providence.

Located just off Athol Island, the Thunderball Reef was the area used to film part of the James Bond movie of the same name. Photo: H. Taylor.

Thunderball is one of the more scenic shallow reef areas around New Providence. A tangle of elkhorn growth provides shelter for numerous small tropicals and even a few lobsters. As the reef is located inside of the Bahamas Marine Park, no lobsters may be taken from the area. Photo: H. Taylor.

The whole reef takes in an area about 100 yards by 35 yards (90 meters by 30 meters). The tops of the coral heads come to within 10 feet (3 meters) of the surface, making it an excellent snorkeling area as well. Hordes of small tropicals crowd the undercuts at the base of the heads, and lobsters can be seen at night.

The shallow bottom, abundant light reflecting off the sand, and fishlife make this a good place to get in some macrophotography. If you look carefully into the crevices and around the edges of the sponges you may see tiny, translucent ghost shrimp, barely large enough to fill a 1:1 macro framer.

Alcora   10

Typical depth range	:	100 ft. (30 m)
Typical current conditions	:	light
Expertise required	:	intermediate to expert
Access	:	boat

Wrecking, or salvaging goods from vessels run up on shallow reefs, was the first major industry in the Bahamas. There are stories that the old-time Bahamian wreckers were not exactly averse to moving warning lights around to make navigation in the shoal-strewn waters around New Providence even chancier. Although the business died out in the 19th century, it seems to be making a comeback of sorts with the advent of scuba diving. The stakes aren't quite as serious, as the "victims" are all derelict vessels and all that's salvaged are good times and photographs. Today's wreckers are the dive operators, who have deliberately put down some of the finest wrecks in the Caribbean. The *Never Say Never Again* wreck on the south side is one. The *Alcora* is another.

This 130-foot (40-meter) ship was confiscated by the Bahamas government and turned over to two diving operators, Underwater Tours and Sun Divers, to dispose of. The only proviso was that they sink it in a place where it wouldn't be a hazard to navigation.

Once used by drug smugglers the Alcora *now carries a cargo of marine life. The vessel was cleaned and stripped of hatches and glass, and deliberately sunk. Photo: H. Taylor.*

There's very little danger of that—it's 80 feet (25 meters) to the deck. Even though the wreck is deep, it's gorgeous. The boat is sitting upright on a sand bottom, surrounded by low, mounding corals.

The ports are open and you can swim through the two large cargo holds in the forward and middle portions of the ship. A light will be needed to penetrate the engine room.

The water over the wreck is often a little murky so, descending through it, you'll at first see nothing but gauzy blue. As you go deeper, the indistinct outlines of the ship begin to form a huge shadow lurking below. Like an amusement park ride, it's a little spooky until the water clears just above the wreck and the entire hull, sitting clean and upright, can be seen.

The operators generally run to the *Alcora* when they have a large enough group of experienced divers to make up a trip. It may be worth mentioning your interest in seeing the wreck early on in your stay, so the operators can more easily find a group qualified to make the dive.

If the *Alcora* is high on your list of diving priorities, contact Joey Lulas at Underwater Tours before you go to New Providence.

French angelfish are among the dozens of species that inhabit the the Alcora *wreck. Since its hatches, doors and glass were removed before it was sunk, the shop is very safe for divers, making it one of the premier wreck dives in the Caribbean.*

Typical depth range	:	10 ft. (3 m)
Typical current conditions	:	light
Expertise required	:	novice
Access	:	boat or beach

Balmoral Island isn't on any dive operator's regular schedule, but it could make a nice outing if you decide to take an afternoon off to snorkel. Particularly for novice snorkelers and children, the area is a terrific introduction to the joys of mask and flippers.

The island is located at the mouth of Goodman's Bay, directly north of the Cable Beach Hotel at Cable Beach.

Balmoral is part of a line of barrier islands that run along the outer reef line of the north shore of New Providence. As such, it has a seaward side and a "lagoon" side. Even when the ocean is a bit rough, there's usually a lee to get away from the swells. The only exception is when the wind blows east to west, sending swells down both sides of the island.

Balmoral Island is part of a chain of barrier islands that run along the outer reef line of the north shore of New Providence. The reef can be clearly seen as the line where the dark blue deep water meets the turquoise of the shallows.

The crystalline, shallow waters of Balmoral Island make a delightful afternoon diversion for snorkelers. Small tropicals, such as this pufferfish, are common on the north side of the island. Particularly for children, it's a good idea to outfit everyone with work gloves. Though you may have trouble finding child-sized gloves, even the overly-large adult sizes are good protection against spines and fire coral. Photo: H. Taylor.

Balmoral is a fair distance from shore, so the best bet is to find a ski boat willing to drop you off and pick you up, or a small boat you can rent for the afternoon. Pull up on the south side, facing shore, and walk across to the ocean side.

The reef line, just offshore, is primarily rocky limestone substrate, with little live coral development. The rocks at the back of the reef harbor an incredible aquarium of small tropicals representing the whole range of Caribbean species.

Bring a lunch and enjoy the privacy. Very few of Nassau's million tourists ever make it to this beautiful little bit of the tropics.

4

Dangerous Marine Life

There aren't many things to worry about while diving around New Providence. The standard Caribbean cautions apply, but even the ubiquitous sea urchins that bedevil the shallow diving of many islands are in short supply here.

Sea urchins. These little long-spined guys look like elaborate pincushions. An essential part of the reef community, urchins graze on algae. They help keep coral healthy by removing algae growths that may settle on a coral's surface and prevent it from feeding.

Backing into or sitting on an urchin may result in the spines puncturing your skin, then breaking off inside. Usually, the reaction is no more than a rash and a little swelling, although some people are more sensitive to spines. After a few days, the spines will dissolve. If they're very bothersome, you might try digging them out with a needle as you would a wood splinter.

Playing with a stonefish is an absolute no-no. The diver here is taking a great risk. The venom contained in the spines of stonefish can cause serious injury or even death.

Fire coral. The most common danger is also the easiest to avoid. Fire coral is not true coral, it's actually a relative of the jellyfish. Fire coral grows over the skeleton of sea fans, encrusts metal objects, and sometimes grows into sheetlike blades standing upright from the bottom. When something, like an unprotected hand, brushes fire coral, small stinging cells called nematocysts inject an irritating chemical into the skin. The resulting rash and burning sensation may last a couple of days.

Most problems with fire coral involve divers backing into it or sitting down on it accidentally. The LCT wreck, for example, is generously coated with fire coral. If you are stung, try rubbing a hydrocortisone first aid cream on the rash, or put some meat tenderizer on it.

Stonefish. Stonefish are members of the scorpionfish family. Aptly named, they look like lumps of algae-covered rock. Generally they just lie on the bottom, so when settling down, check to see that the rocks around you are, in fact, rocks. The spines just forward of the stonefish's dorsal fin can inject a powerful poison if they puncture the skin.

Fire coral may look like a regular coral colony, or it may be found as an encrusting growth on a wreck, on rocks, or even on sea fans. Wherever you find it, keep your distance. The rash it causes isn't serious, but it is annoying. Photo: H. Taylor.

Moray eels. There are some gigantic green morays hiding in the reefs around New Providence. Like most other things in the sea, they aren't really dangerous unless you insist on harassing them. It's a good idea to keep your hands out of dark crevices under the reef. You may stick your hand in a hole and pull it back with an eel attached to it. If you do see an eel, it won't hurt to examine it from a respectful distance, but if the eel decides to retreat, it's best to let it go.

Sharks. Sharks are everywhere. However, some places have fewer sharks than others, and New Providence is one of these. You're not likely to see anything but nurse sharks in the shallows of the north side or south side. There are some pelagic sharks, such as hammerheads, on the more isolated sections of the south side. Spearing fish with scuba is against the law here anyway, so divers have little to fear from any stray sharks they may encounter.

Rays. There are a fair number of rays around New Providence. Rays, once called "devilfish" by sailors, are not really devilish at all. Like stonefish, they mostly lie on the bottom minding their own business. However, they don't care to be stepped on, sat on, or prodded. The sharp barb near the base of the tail can inflict a very deep and painful wound. One diver who accidentally stepped on a ray and was hit in the leg likened it to getting shot with a .22 caliber rifle.

Bristle worms are also called fire worms. Like fire coral, brushing against one could result in a burning sensation, usually followed by a slight rash. The best treatment is hydrocortisone cream. Photo: H. Taylor.

The small lump at the base of this stingray's tail is the stinger. Rays are very docile and are only dangerous if they're kicked, prodded, or sat on. As this ray demonstrates, the animals are sometimes hard to distinguish from the scrabble of a patch reef.

5

Safety

The diving operators on New Providence are conscientious about their customers. They'll be more than happy to assist you in any way to make your diving safer and more fun.

Ultimately, however, your personal safety is your responsibility. Listen closely to dive guides and instructors, and follow their directions. Also be aware of what your options are, or aren't, during each dive. If you don't remember how to use the dive tables, ask for help. You'll look a whole lot less foolish getting help with the tables before a dive than you will having to ask for emergency help afterwards.

Chambers. Information on chambers and treatment facilities is offered here only as a convenience. Because the status and location of hyperbaric chambers changes, we cannot be responsible for the accuracy of information. We strongly suggest you get the information you need before leaving the U.S., and write it in a place that's accessible while you're diving, such as in your dive log.

The closest emergency chamber is in Grand Bahama. The closest full service chamber is in Miami, an hour's flight away. In case of an accident, there are two places you can call. The first is the Bahamas Air Sea Rescue, or BASRA. Their number is 809-322-3877 or 325-3743. The second is the Diver's Alert Network.

DAN, the **Diver's Alert Network**, is a membership association of individuals and organizations sharing a common interest in diving safety. DAN operates a **24-hour national hotline (919) 648-8111** (collect calls are acepted in an emergency). DAN does not provide medical care, although they do provide advice on early treatment, evacuation, and hyperbaric treatment of diving related injuries. Additionally, DAN provides diving safey information to help prevent accidents. Membership is $10 a year, and includes: the DAN *Underwater Diving Accident Manual*, describing symptoms and first aid for the major diving related injuries; emergency room physician guidelines for drugs and i.v. fluids; a membership card listing diving related symptoms on one side and

DAN's emergency and non-emergency phone numbers on the other; one tank decal and three small equipment decals with DAN's logo and emergency number; and a newsletter, "Alert Diver," which describes diving medicine and safety information in layman's language with articles for professionals, case histories, and medical questions related to diving. Special memberships for dive stores, dive clubs, and corporations are also available. The DAN Manual can be purchased for $4 from the Administrative Coordinator, National Diving Alert Network, Duke University Medical Center, Box 3823, Durham, NC 27710.

DAN divides the U.S. into seven regions, each coordinated by a specialist in diving medicine who has access to the skilled hyperbaric chambers in his region. Non-emergency or information calls are connected to the DAN office and information number (919) 684-2498. This number can be dialed direct between 9 a.m. and 5 p.m. Monday through Friday, Eastern Standard Time. Divers should *not* call DAN for chamber locations in advance. Chamber status changes frequently, making this kind of information dangerous if it's obsolete at the time of an emergency. Instead, divers should contact DAN as soon as a diving emergency is suspected. DAN can then give advice on the nearest operating facility able to handle the emergency. All divers should have comprehensive medical insurance and check to make sure that hyperbaric treatment and air ambulance services are covered internationally.

Diving is a safe sport, and there are few accidents compared to the number of divers and number of dives made every year. But when the infrequent injury does occur, DAN is ready to help. DAN, originally 100 percent federally funded, is now largely supported by the diving public. Membership in DAN or purchase of DAN manuals or decals provides divers with safety information and provides DAN with necessary operating funds. Donations to DAN are tax deductible as DAN is a chartered non-profit public service organization.

Index